D1041062

TOTEM POLES
AND RAILROADS

TOTEM POLES

POLES

&

RAILROADS

BY

JANET

ROGERS

ARP Books (Arbeiter Ring Publishing)
201E-121 Osborne Street
Winnipeg, Manitoba
Canada R3L 1Y4
arpbooks.org

Cover artwork by Sonny Assu
We Come To Witness, 2014
Digital intervention on an Emily Carr Painting (Silhouette No. 2, 1930)
Image courtesy of the Artist.

Book design and layout by Sébastien Aubin.
Printed and bound in Canada by Friesens on paper made from
100% recycled post-consumer waste.

Second printing, October 2017.

ARP Books acknowledges the generous support of the Manitoba Arts Council and the Canada Council for
the Arts for our publishing program. We acknowledge the financial support of the Government of Canada
through the Canada Book Fund and the Province of Manitoba through the Book Publishing Tax Credit and
the Book Publisher Marketing Assistance Program of Manitoba Culture, Heritage, and Tourism.

Library and Archives Canada Cataloguing in Publication
Rogers, Janet Marie, 1963-, author
        Totem poles and railroads / Janet Rogers.
Poems.
ISBN 978-1-894037-87-7 (paperback)
        I. Title.
PS8585.O395158T68 2016   C811'.6   C2016-905008-4

CONTENTS

BODY OF SONG	LAURA SECORD
RED EARTH, WHITE LIES	HOW DO YOU SAY MONEY?
THE PEOPLE	THE SPIRIT OF RADIO INDIGENOUS
SLOW BURN	LEMME SEE YA DANCE
WE ARE ALL MICHAEL BROWN	POCAHANTAS
HUMAN DYNAMIC ACTIVITY	
WHERE ARE YOUR GUTS?	ANTECEDENT
PROCLAMATION	BEARS REPEATING
WHO DO YOU THINK YOU ARE?	RECKLESS
HUMAN RIGHTS	
I WAS HERE, WERE YOU?	DON VALLEY
THERE IS A RECORD EXISTS	
MAKE SOUND	416
BOWEL. MY ANSWER TO HOWL	
DECEMBER	YONGE AND COLLEGE
CALLS TO ACTION	THIS IS A POEM FOR NINA SIMONE
TOTEM POLES AND RAILROADS	FINAL REPORT
SACAJAWEA	MUSH HOLE
DAKOTA DREAMING	SHAHSI'TO:WANE The Big Footed One
GREAT LAW	BEAR LOVE

BODY

sliding multiples
running wave visuals
currents swelling
telling ocean stories
making harmonies
and movements
ancient ingredients
predating humans
we are tapping
into something
instinctual rituals
one magic

Hummmmmmmmmmmm

a sonic

Ommmmmmmmmmmmm

trills on the tongue
Lalalalalalalalala
calling our gods
come play
first body song
echoes in ripples

t-t-t-t triples

penetrating silence
leading not forcing
our instruments together
orbiting sensual
breath of life
lingering in memory
no use rejecting
harmonies piercing

our hearts
opening the closings
filling in the blanks
answers and deep knowing

our universal YESSSSS

bass tones
gravitational notes
holding souls
whole body stone
give it up to alto
let in soprano
melodies keeping us
dreaming releasing

Whey-ah-hey-hey-ya

SONG

super genius compositions
song creations easy as breathing
handmade homespun woven notes
dancing on debris
knowing eight generations
join us in chorus
we hear them and name them
without words they tell us
to sing like the river
pouring our souls into
every syllable
exhausting and elevating
stacking our voices and expanding
collective consciousness
Hu-Hu-Hu-Hu-Hu-Hu...

born from air
ethereal sound perfume
stays with you
long after the glow
trans-portal transmissions
serving love's purpose
blessings natural and indescribable
it just is
songs and sounds and notes
and sounds and notes and songs
and notes and songs and sounds
and songs and sounds and notes
and sounds and notes and songs
and songs and songs and bodies
and songs

RED EARTH

new world born from myth
scientific rejected creation stories
christian notations and bible fiction
inflexible spiritual doctrines
of discovery

original oral indigenous   inferior
missionary religious slogans superior
the discomfort
so intolerable
to cultivate a land bridge theory   so
impossible
to justify
factual atrocities built   here
from a foundation   of theories

bering strait equates to B.S.
red earth white lies
caucasoid
asia to alaska
army corp of america
holding and controlling
DNA from nine thousand
years ago

balloon like conclusions
floating up in the *one* direction
never considered
say some

we rested in new mexico
by way of chile
sounds like a fine
vacation after a long day's journey
following mammoths
and other hard won meat
when abundant vegetation
right under our feet should
go overlooked

interior routes examined and disputed
considering coastal cultures with canoes
looking to australia with avant-garde seafood
appetites and waves of abundance
chasing nothing but discovery

without solid evidence scientists
have early man travelling by leaps
of faith across impassable
lands of early Yupik bands
now a national park
peace treaty territory
where russia and america
shook hands in a land heist
claiming shared heritage
and naming their adopted baby
beringina
displaced scientists themselves
in need of origin stories

DEBUNKING BERING STRAIT

WHITELIES

unless they have descended from
mysterious sources
crossing fictional terrain
following dinosaurs over cliffs
finding flight
too late

mongoloid ice age migrants
without status or governance
theorists debunked and cut loose
scratching out our Creator's name
religion and science tag-team wrestling
remnants of asian cultures
propaganda taught as fact
defending theories and rejecting evidence
as a matter of fact and fact as matter
like a smoking gun
in a cop's hand stood over
black youth
you want truth

how they love to tell me where I'm from
sat comfortably from places named after
kings and princes who never even visited
stinging insults to those who reference it
by nature's names
ignoring obvious evidence as if

what do you mean
"Go back from where you came "

emphasized with ridiculous hyphenated
exaggeration
paleo-Indian, aboriginal-north american
putting people before place
tagging regions
with pronunciations twisting our tongues
as Vine Deloria said
bering strait is short for
"I don't know"
good stories though
making it up as they go
I am writing
new histories
absent of
white lies
from this
brown face

THE
PEOPLE

the viper's kryptonite is alcohol
greed-induced dreams
drunken benders of lies
super powers and abused words
rhetorical rhetoric
from dead-faced soldiers
intoxicated sailors
misreading charts
following courses
into oncoming storms
last minute decisions
and overgrown pride
taking over qualities resembling
humanity
compassion
reason even

we wake to a new day
and show fear where it can leave
we are inspired and see clear
the soul-sick individuals
the misguided Windigo
baby boys crying for mommy
throw away war's spoils
make friends
we are a victimless nation
a powerhouse of answers
more potent than policy
more real than paper
guided by our celestial
connections

S L O W

where family language
was spoken
often
listen as
ghost words surface
revealed along midnight's tide

Salish syllable sounds
decorate swelling clouds
here spirit knowledge is practiced
it strikes like
fires that cleanse
tears transformed to
precious land lessons
before territories
traded for fortunes
stolen

ornamental butterfly
   slow burn
grand fur
   chocolate lily
Indian celery
   white head   iron wood
ocean spray
   whale vertebrae
poisons
   medicines
         slow burn

trade relations
define cultural connections
descriptive liquid harvest
salivating nature
divided by stories
memories and manmade
histories

                  slow burn

white-capped answers
extended backwards
in time the cries

of hunger burn holes
through thick mist
kissing and caressing

water waking
skin relations
move in unison
flowing up
descending down
flowing up
descending down
flowing
up
up
up

oregon grape
                  arbutus root

Indigenous yellow dye

                           slow burn

pit cook   eel grass

                  digging black ash

reverse falls
here Xa:ls
casts food in directions
foreign
hidden middens
time travellers
vibrational energies collecting
moving through
bottleneck wreckage
it seems so long ago

it was just then
and now
and here

                  slow burn

BURN

WE
ARE
ALL
MICHAEL
BROWN

my eyes are dark clouds
heavy with rain
my stomach is a tree trunk
moving syrup to my heart
mixing liquid light
passion and pain
flowing through veins
bleeding answers
follow us
we are found face down
on cold concrete
from the comfort of a bucket-seat
we are hunted like game
my words must be rhymes
to your reason
truth to power potent hope
drains like rain into sewers
my eyes now open
inside the heart
hears nothing
silence has moved in
we are made of nature
evil lives here too
I saw my niece today
in the face of a beautiful
brown girl
and pretended it was her
standing by the water
ready to rescue us
surely she knows
I am just flesh
and eyes and stomach
and heart
I am a fist
I am choice
my hands are solar panels
to praise and release
I am reaching deep
inside healing
feeling the burn
this is a young man's answer
to his mother saying
"Never grow old"

HUMAN
DYNAMIC
ACTIVITY

seven sacred cycles
completed
transcendence
of oppression
high energy vibrations
decolonized mindfulness
meditate daily
built-in resistance
sit in repose
manifest destiny
school books
more powerful
than a bible
a bible less than law

1824, 1830, 1970

our courts are in just us
looms over us
concurred dispossessed
moved on
liberation follows
repatriation
bankrupt
idealism
social work different
from savior work
rebirth and self-reliance
disease-free bodies
are bodies free of

intra-fear-rants
retrain the brain
re-learn the original
we are not the Kardashians
we are healers
testimony in ceremony
urban-outfitters marketing
smudge sticks complete with
prayer manuals available
online

empathy with the inanimate
is advanced and decolonized
mindfulness
difference and separation
forms in primal lobe
dissolved with song
repetitive repetitive
singing with nature
repetitive
until we are together
vibrating together
human dynamic activity

Human dynamic activity
Say it
Human dynamic activity
Say it

WHERE

where are your guts
coiled up inside your middle
holding vigil
lying in wait
before striking and hissing
cobra-like for the next
insult to culture and self

have you found your voice
a sound unique and dangerous
a little embarrassing
upon playback
disbelief lives on the skin
rises like goosebumps
suspended drama not written
but lived as honesty
bringing us face to face
with mortality
alien disturbance
annoying and incredibly
frightening
coming close
closer than usual
trust your guts

YOUR

ARE

don't forget
and constantly remember
be grateful
we have hands to give thanks
our feet leave tracks
I will light this fire
and call it sacred
silence is the fragrance
holding nature's essence
that calms the body
and awakens our senses
we haven't yet named it
so there is no claim

come lay with me
show me your guts
and hold my hand
there

GUTS?

all language
is emotional
passion lives
inside compassion
proclamations of home
and heart
real
as hunger
and
love

something
as expansive
as the blank
page
never shifts
from caucasian
protagonist
playing both
hero
and victim

in triangulations
jockeying for position
an academic sport
treating each moment
like a photo op

there will
always be
things we don't
know
a secret
a lesson
a lie
awaiting liberation

whole histories of this

violence
is the language
of unintelligence
a child conceived
in fear and sadness
methods to assert
superiorities
the negotiations
never go well

genius is he
who invented
alcohol and guns
setting the stage
where no good
can come

an eye for an eye
crying kept
in private
the purging
of feelings
are small
victories
personal and
inevitable
we mime our meanings
and speak the language
of tears
as post script

PROCLA-
MATION

new seasons see
brown-skinned lovers
touch each other
their reflections
meet in the middle

the birds have returned
in numbers greater
they never pour
over politics
or separate major from minor
their notes are constant
and resonate as equals
natural soundtracks
to a world gorging itself
on importance

the lovers leave
with seasons new
followed by ghosts
who gave up so much
for their love
to blossom
where are you?
creative energies
orbiting minority voices
like legends
existing as twice removed
creation stories
perpetuating
separateness

countries
built by oppressive
minds manipulating
who do they think
you are?
in this new season
when what we say
and what we be
join hands briefly
in make-believe
marriage
brought together
by hurt feelings
healing is intellectual
fodder
with glaring absence
of emotion
true and essential
self-definitions
hold space
make up
new definitions
never existing
without academic
validations

think
don't believe
what do you know
about me?
what do you mean?
what do I mean?
who do you think
you are?

W H O
D   O
Y O U
THINK
Y O U
A R E ?

a wise woman once said
don't be foolish
you have no rights
no one was present upon
your birth
holding a certificate
of rights
those who travelled here
in 1492 and henceforth
made their rights, right
they write the laws
we are forced to follow
and took it even further
taking and making the right
to control the lives of others
enslavement of a people
the concept so absurd
going against religious doctrines
they themselves claim
to defend and enact
can you imagine that?

there is no equality
a fallacy taught to you and me
so we keep our dreams tamed
the aim is not to strive to be equal
but to be the best
perhaps superior to another
there is no equal
only the best we all can be
we live in this commitment
a tangible energy action behavior
we confuse the land beneath us
with our titles and make believe
no equality without rights for all
no rights for all
not without my say so
for me
when I am free
you look free to me
too

HUMA

RIGH

there is no settler nation
only immigrants of generations
this title trickery doesn't work on me
labeling me minority
visibility only you can see
when you see me lesser than you
saying I live in the margins of this society
stop lying without me there is no you
what is racist?
a rippling question
shape-shifting since those ships arrived
prisons are the new plantations
prisons are the new reserves
rehabilitation of the body and mind
we no longer let you mess with our rights
the commodification of our cultures
stops now
hating us while making a profit from us
what kind of fucked-up disconnected/pimp
thinking/white-extremist/ blood-sucking/
devil-worshipping/money-sick/ hill-billy
shit is this?

what's worse?
racist activism from within
what a thing?
I've seen ally-ships go all
kinds of ways wrong
never open that mic
or offer the floor
you can bet the time and space
will be stolen
don't cry settler
be proud
of your history
you have the names of your people
written on your face
you have the honour
of carrying on a legacy
without ownership
you are the new poster child
of canadian

N

TS

I
WAS
HERE,
WERE
YOU?

are you the edible flower
dried in hot July sunshine
steeped for six minutes
poured over foreign porcelain
smuggled inside steamer trunks
leaving european ports
for new york shores
processing people surviving sicknesses
restless sleepless
migratory transmissions
controlling policies
unhappy circumstances in search of
affluence and abundance
advertised in thick-paper
publications evoking
reluctant discussions
expectant spouses
fighting about meager existences
saving apple crates to sit on
inside cold-water walk-ups
where rent is paid
three days late
and kitchen sink
haircuts fail to impress
because the accent's too thick
and looks can kill
inside overcrowded buses
travelling in opposite directions
of destinations
where underinflated
paychecks wait in locked boxes
carefully calculated by
skinny-fingered accountants who never change their outfits sucking on peppermint toothpicks
not even on Sundays or holidays
like lent giving up free chocolate
and crusty breads leaving crumbs
for back porch pigeons
scratching messages
into wooden platforms
with symbols saying

"I was here, Were you?"

THERE

IS A

RECORD

EXISTS

did she really speak?
asked only as a courtesy
of something that lives as certainty
in my bones
although many may doubt
those familiar and close
understand the gift
this connection and visit
passing through worlds
to hear a voice so missed .
to know her tone
her rich instrument
her passport and tool
representing to deliver
biting reflections served
inside cups of honey
drink it up
with a wink and a kick
her potions churning up history
to an audience of canadians
but sing she didn't
poetic lyrics spoken with theatrics
enough to woo them
dressed in lace gowns
iridescent pearls decorating her cocoa-
coloured throat
shoulders free to swivel
pointing her true breast
towards house-left
instinctual gestures
raising her voice in emotional verse

potent pro-woman stories
men feigning disgust
disguising their lust
sisters sitting on their sense of empowerment
inspired by answers she spins in verse
calling out oppression and prejudice
she held freedom in her heart
paying attention to the times
and playing the game expertly
male travel companions
beards really bearded men
writing letters of introductions
never forging signatures of dignitaries
but implying closeness
out of necessity of acceptance
living a bit outside of it
as creativity required it
to keep being her
sipping tea and shooting whiskey
with the best of them
queen bees line themselves
along her windowsill
to speak a language
only understood by her
seeping into her dreams
upon waking frantic transcriptions
find their way to the page
atop a rickety desk in the
quiet of early morning
bathed in a temperate light
filtered by watching trees

lined outside the house
rhymes coming easy
words threaded together like
charms on a bracelet
she speaks them aloud
to measure compatibility
never compromising matter
for art but steeping beauty
from a boiling passion
who do you write for Miss Pauline?
the crown to whom your family
pledged their undying loyalties
your grandfather Smoke keeper
of family wampum a historical honesty
the children you never had
and never missed
the community who both rejected and
revered
the immigrant side so easily impressed
with tricks of memory
the brown ones now so proud
our oration not imitation of
captains and colonels
inspiration for the troupes
it is you
making connections
forging alliances as poet ambassador
such a powerful position
for a woman
claiming this nation
owning it all

we enter her home
and meekly speak
we read each poem
from their proud place of origin
with exhilaration
we call her come forth
and she weighs
an informal invitation
from a contented spirit place
she looks upon the ladies
crying in her parlour
walking her halls
and talking about a duality
guilty we are all
reality a two-faced mirror
born into nature's arms with gifts
and privilege she paved a path
to ensure its foundation with
repetition
she has come back
like Sky Woman
and lives on a little inside every one
we see her in the land
and along the Grand
she speaks in a tone of a time
that is equal of her
I know this
because I heard her

make sound
imprint this
on the memory
of the enemy

choose words
carefully
never forget
the dreams
in abstract images
and messages
in sound

look
them in the eye
let them see
courage
and conviction
look them in the eye
see uncertainty
rooted just behind
their hard stare

get close
close enough
to sense
injustice
feel what it
feels like
so we know
what it feels like
when we feel it
again

let them
arrest us
so the visual
of our beautiful
bound together
impacts memory
touches them
in the subconscious
help them

with soul memory
when we walk
earth's surface
beside each other
we live this dignity
awakened again
large as mountain beings
connected to stars
recalling our songs
our sounds

KE
UND

BOWEL

TO HOWL

hot tears roll
a forced letting go
critical gaze upon my
discontented soul
turns up in published
words

deeper the poet's needs
are deeper her voice deeper
language fuller with meaning
faster logic and loose words
mad-crazy like jazz
and getting high
sudden and unexpected
death

what are we doing?
letting strangers
into our psyche
this is not conquest
it is ego and ambition
taming itself
with inauthentic intimacy
we are not our successes
not really

I can no longer stomach
public vigils pretending
to be something
I don't wear ribbons
or sign petitions
or make stupid
useless statements
about countries
where I've never been
and know nothing about

there is no beat generation
just rejection of convention
bodies, breathing rhythms
feeling the highs and lows
our brothers and sisters
bringing their best confessions
and burning them in the glow

we're all so thirsty
for the same simple things
I can't name what you are
to me
I can't please you until
you see you in me

there is no escape
although we make
literary attempts
that dump purpose
call bullshit on
dishonest
please don't waste my time

undesirable notions
keep poking my ribs
superfluous voices live inside
pillows where your head
holds them in

activists discovering new angst
to perpetuate identity
fixated on the one thing
that equates to discriminate

this is culture
this is uncooked food

if only the invasion of ill-conceived children
was debated the same way as
refugees and immigration
what's all the hoopla
about reproduction anyway

bricks scraping skies
informing personalities
giving definition
to whole societies
hand built with
masculinity
holding territories
being held
in place
with time

with ten percent
human brain activity
can we define
heart-break
girl parts boys' hearts
making up new words
to describe sub-arctic

don't condemn the artist
for misinterpreting the muse
relevance and speculation
live in the same neighborhood
forever is a long time...sigh...timeless

recompose or decompose

hair growth is a measure
from one phase to another
overexposure
be real with me
build bonfires with me

Y lives beside T
and when I can't sleep
I mind-type names and stories
all a ploy to get to
the source
nothing stays stagnant forever
that's a long long time...remember?

deliberation of guilt
must be followed by
reason and rationale
forced choices
made autonomous
first with the heart
then with the mind
rejected by logic
just walk it off

strong words hesitate
in the bulb of my brow
indecisive and insecure words
learn-ed words
luscious and righteous words
soothing balms and medicines

we are always emotional
love is an animal
be sure to feed it
and give it plenty of water
we survive our feelings daily
and asked to provide
proof of life upon waking
with ten percent
human brain activity
can you define
self

something
is tugging
on my earlobe
feels like
change
is coming
yet I hear nothing

this goes on
for three days or so
muscle spasms
on the face forcing
aged expressions
reflections
from within

I speak
in every way
my body can
to convey
keeping my mouth shut
holding verbal worlds hostage
not the usual practice

these symbolic
acts of honor
patriotism
in half-mast flags
leave images
and archetypes
for dreamtime
speak little
leave room to listen

there is
a time for intensity
and a place
to express it
there is
a time for calm
contented periods
but this isn't it

evoking spirit
through ritual
with reason
quotations
around the words
"heart, head
and stomach"
mean something

I am taking
my time
and some of yours
I am connecting
to energies
respectfully
staying
with it
genuinely

it is December again
frenzied activities
destroying focus
swinging at anything
calling the ball
low and inside

DECE

removing
negativity like a surgeon
striking great big X's
all over old scripts
no turkey
no trimmings
endings are beginnings
learning words
in the language
i:wehre entsorihwase'ne
it becomes popular again

determination
thick as a dictionary
ignoring schematics
knowing sometimes
the damage we do
is good
it's worth it
pouring
gasoline all over
resolutions
to see what survives

a sentimental life
is the opposite of
a plastic plant
you gotta
grow that thing
from scratch
take your time
keep it real
with me

watch
as a new year
approaches
promises
of changes
and new advancements
as needed

MBER

CALLS
TO
ACTION
BR-UMP-BUMP

looking to the left
then right
positioning ourselves
somewhere in this redress
patching up our wounds
like road crews
in the commission of truth
merging and making square
armed with these calls
to action

numbered requests
so many suggestions
prescriptions all beginning with
"We call upon the federal, provincial,
territorial and aboriginal governments..."

equalizing compensation
busted k-k-kanadians
remedies for the malaise
restoring stripped dignity
upon territories by eradicating
the spanking law
that's all

monitoring our own neglect
administering our own medicines
handling the sliding scale
and setting new precedents
and measurements
for success

authoring treaties and dissolving
two-way for four-way portals
with language and culture
including clauses for noncompliance
prison term punishment
let's try it

all things defined by adequate funding
have we learned nothing
but how to correspond in dollars
with the white-man
for over time
what we find to be adequate
will inevitably evolve
as will this law
no land no advancements
no chance for balance
only more hand-outs
who do we make the cheque out to

the U. N. Declaration reads as
un-declare lets pump the brakes here
Indigenous rights
a meaningless concept
absent of commitment
a signature-less contract
"R" words left flapping
like tattered flags
over parliament's decaying
brick home

Rights   rights   Reconcile
reconcile
Response response   Relocate   relocate

D is for independent decisions
and safe drinking water
E expressions of interest
and evolving realities

winter olympics actually
sited as successful relations
unprecedented four-host first nations
get our regalia on and dance for the good
people
contributions to the
larger cultural national fabric

larger cultural national fabric
.

upon closer examination
the garment is frayed and worn
patched with miss-matched fabrics
darning them together
damning it forever
too little too late

drums and feathers
the new black and brown
incantations and chants
environmental tourism
omits a history eliminated
by name changes
singing in ceremonies
for your listening enjoyment
our employment

.

a collective dream and shotgun wedding
a nightmare written in legalese
still calling on the crown
to join pen to paper
royal proclamations
adopting Indigenous laws   never
agreements with the master
diamond encrusted collars   still choking

spiritual self-determination
hot lava-beds of policymaking
creation stories taught as myth
not bible books but oral legacies
the way it was meant to be
misinterpretations to suit the seasons

we are the rich fine wine
improving with age
improving health
improving negotiations
demanding the pope's apology
funding museums
and the canadian federation
of 2017
one hundred and fifty
years of deceased school children
buried treasures in unmarked graves

TRC of canada
I trust a TRC of mafia more
there may be no honour among thieves
at least their treaties
come with a time line
and a no-fault clause
honour?
our honour?
how much
does that cost?

TOTEM POLES AND RAILROADS

early foggy
cups of coffee
six miles of slippery
frost hugging
everything
nothing escapes
raven's gaze
no need to speed
sharp focus both
comfort and mysterious

missing faces
smiling
from weather worn
big wide billboards
counting days to months to tears
open season
for truckers and policemen

"Wouldn't you want to clear yourself
of suspicion?"

inhabitants eat well here
until the kindness of
stranger-neighbours dries up
like ice after November
presence and economics
played like lazy hands
of poker
not in our favour
numbers don't lie
paranoia is colonial
arriving on foreign ships of deceit
landing on honest shores
of indigenous innocence

my eyes rapid scan bears women
red-stained shoulders
raven's pecking order
in the rearview mirror
each territory has a centre
and signal to follow suit
change reverberates
heritage stagnates
politics holds road blocks to progress

resolution
perpetuation
penetrations

altered consciousness evolved
best we stay awake
authenticity burgeoning
fresh reality crossing
potholes and holy practices

deep hibernation
this is the winter
of our discounts
tobacco placed
another season buried
snow and time
evidence can provide
remembering releasing
beginning healing
hunting down haunting
a harvest of honest
traumatic brutality
sickness reflecting flesh ripping
steel vehicles
extractions
          extractions
                    extractions

low cloud cover
thirty more days
skid marks and hitchhikers
swerving listening for voices
nothing
none of this is ours
propaganda is the first tool

totem poles and railroads
canada post diesel and drugs
uncomfortable with discomfort
everything is human error
pointing towards police

cop cars passing
opposite directions
I look to them like
I know something
like they know something
and not saying
we are not sure
what's been saved
or deleted

and there she is...
heated cheeks
slack jacket slung
from half a mile back
body language exhausted
walking south
I want my finger in her face
shake and say
don't you dare
just don't
just don't
do it

the precipice of heaven high mountains
stately Carolina angels
singing raw rich notes
filling souls with authentic sermons
uplifts this heavy energy
hearts beating slower
still inspired
proclamations of beauty
we'll know now
and round dance
all the possibilities

museums and tractor sculptors
monuments of extraction culture
not the threat of natural distractions
but the other guy
breaking at eighty forcing urgency
to all things caution
clearing the passenger's side
everything has shifted
new conversations and concerns

not my territory
I can't ask the ancestors
for anything
directions change from east to north
feel gut rocks dissolve
a happier road
Indian road
I know this road
paved for commerce as commodity
with little return
backwards running river
no more road
I won't stop
not for cops

I AM NOT NEXT

eight lovely degrees
at the end of October
birch bark stark white
furs are furrier
eyes peeled
more giving thanks
totem poles and railroads
mountain houses
names of princes
borrowed bored cancer spots
small town slumm'n
I would not insult them
to call them
ghosts
they are here
voiceless moons
reflecting heat
travel companions reaching
destinations at last
done with victim rhetoric
scientists of our own circumstances
architects of resistance
facts flooding highways
mudslides and
construction zones

slow
            stop
                go

My young eyes saw many unusual and exciting
things.
A life full of random circumstance.
I decided to see each one as an adventure, lest I
bury myself in pity.
I must have been preoccupied the day the
captors came.
The skilled huntsmen grabbed all but a few and
slaughtered the rest.
My brothers, my parents, near all my friends,
dead, disappeared.
What was I to do?
I had skills mind you.
Not enough to keep myself alive, alone.
There was nothing left of my village.
I was taken along trails leading to another
camp.
They made me work.
I worked all day.
I was still a girl then.
The ache in my heart so great I was numb to my
own needs and wants.
Without my family and community it was hard
to say who I was.
I couldn't be anything really. I was
underdeveloped and no one to teach me.
I was fed, enough to work, all the day and into
night.
I saw the world around me in a new light.
I spoke only to my own soul and it spoke back
to me.
The Indian women from that place treated me
less than a pet.
I belonged to everyone and yet no one.
I was a beautiful maiden.
I did not have freedom.
My mind and spirit was my only true territory.
My body was another thing.
My heart lay dead with my people
There was nothing more to take.

It was absolute and unequivocal, blind and
dumb luck
that won me to be the possession of the
Frenchman.
I observed how the others disrespected him
and thought him dim.
The Frenchman himself orphaned and
transplanted.
Lost most everything with his ill skilled
wagering.
His hunting knives, his beaver pelts, a gold
tooth found in another camp.
Luck blew in on a breeze and passed over his
hands.
That's how he won me.
We could never speak.
In fact he didn't even like me.
He barely turned his eyes to me.
But I was his.
And it was up to me to feed us both.
Whatever he wanted, whatever his needs.
The others didn't concern themselves
with his cruelty or perversity.
I had no one to tell my troubles to
and no time to twist over my sorrows.
Behind my tired eyes there was only blank
discomfort.
I missed the memories of pictures.
Faces of my friends in full natural colours .
Over time, I couldn't recall anything special of
their features.
Like slowly going blind and using extra senses
to survive.

SACAJAWEA

There was always lots of talking.
All they did was talk-talk talking.
Like constant rain unable to make it stop.
They came to me to say gather your things.
My Frenchman was chosen, but really it was me
they wanted to help traverse the complex
relations into far-off places.
The pale ones had a serious plan and they liked
my brown tan and fair face.
Soon into the venture I awarded them another,
something they saw as
a virtue to their cause.
My baby was born a half-French full joy son.
He came to me in the spring and there was
never any question of him joining in.
The pale ones loved him and I never let the
Frenchman touch him.
Wrapped in soft cloth a gift from Lewis or was
it Clarke?
My baby never left me, along windy rivers and
rugged cliffs, I held him tight to me.

The travelling party grew and shrank with the
hardships of our voyage.
I knew I was trusted, I knew to trust too.
At the end of each day, they sat to scratch
symbols on the page.
I watched and crinkled my nose in the same
way.
Mocking them and pretending to do as they do.
The black man, York was his name. A servant to
Clarke or was it Mister Lewis?
The one who too lost all, was the closest thing
to a friend.
I made the crinkle nose face to him. He made it
back to me.
Looking over to the white guys making sure
we'd get it right until one of us burst
into laughter.
Of this game we never grew tired.

Then sickness so severe.
Hot, hot faces, swords in the stomach.
Stopping all progress.
No passage for two days.
The men took my baby when I dropped.
They seemed to really like him.
Made toys from twigs and gave him rations.
Conversing with hands and actions when we
had to.
I learned to raise my shoulders and drop them
when I didn't understand.
My Frenchman chirpped hastily around the
others saying unkind things about me.
I don't think they believed him. His words were
never followed by action.
That's when I learned how useless all the talk
was.
He knew drips and drops of my words, but
refused to speak them.
My black friend had less than that.
He was never consulted or questioned.
That black man was an island and I constantly
tried to read him.

There was dancing.
Silly quirky dancing that sprang from dead
exhaustion when the fiddle kicked in.
Their stringed kitten never purred on my ears.
I enjoyed the boys tossing their bodies together
in linked arms and lifted boots.
They danced when things were good.
When they won a hoard of horses.
Full bellies from a big hunt.
I never joined in, Frenchman wouldn't let me.
Instead I listened, and watched and giggled.
Learned the strange words to their songs.
They danced on long after I laid my head to
rest.
There was no need for me to celebrate one day
to the next.
I had my work, my purpose to prove.
Their plan was my plan and I too wanted to see
the ocean on the other side.
I wondered what the wide open spaces
promised.
Maybe an escape maybe someone new.

I was the original all over the place Indian.
Stolen, sold, traded, adopted, rejected, broken.
The men chased the thrill of discovery and
recognitions from their kings and gods.
I wanted to keep going, simply searching for self.
Hoping to find hope again.
My small son, what could I possibly offer him?
I never doubted creators plan but from time to time
would wonder;

Where the hell are my songs!!!!!!
Why can't I dance too??????

What has them gripped?
Gorging on dogs and horses.
Packing furniture along terrain so tough no
animal sees fit to stay.
No game. They starved close to death and
cursed the nature they could not concur.
The fog must descend.
And we must wait.
In the end it was an Anglicized version of my
own name, intertwined with them.
I took the whole side of my story to the grave.
I gave my son to the white one for promises of
comfort and education.
I knew nothing of these things and nothing to
disobey.
By sea I returned east, left the Frenchman for
an English one.
Left him and followed one more.
Nothing to lose or gain.
No home so I kept going.
All the statues of me stand as symbols of my
soul-less resilience.
Now I rest in a map-less heaven, and travel
down rivers where I am guide to no one.
No knowledge of descendants left behind.
No knowledge how my boy survived.

They called me many things throughout the
years but not one got it right.
A name lost, leaving me to spin anchorless upon
an earth.
Sag-a-jewah, Sag-a-jeweeha, Saj-ga-weeh.
A musical remembrance of a tumultuous
journey.
A life defined by luck and pity.

where sky is king
where clouds rule
where rain waves
a wet scepter over the city
where airplanes
are set free
where the mighty
mississippi
married anishnabe
where the sun shows all
where light and dark
concede in a draw
where sister spirits
speak up
break down
peer round pillars
where we remember
to ask permission
where we commit acts
of protocol
where little earth
and AIM laid claim
where snows found
nowhere to land
so they just keep falling
where flour
has two meanings
where train and tracks
seldom stop
where old and new
come together making
a culture called hipster
where land is lost
to valleys and lakes
where fish defend
their right to swim
where church bells
peel and fade
and wake the dead
where tired comes to rest
where the masons methods

DAKOTA

DREAMING

are built in brick
this is where
soft fawn-skinned
women touch
toe to earth
where they lay
where they pray
where eastern energy
is everywhere
where silence says
"give it a try"
where demolitions
produce beauteous ruins
where babies
lay sleeping
in cumulous bounty
this is where
headwaters
pour generous
where righteous
indigenous
made handshake
agreements
where scandinavian
names remain
where twins divide
rather than bind
where black star blankets
river locks
and Tater-Tots
here a recipe was born
at four in the morn
the unknown
bring visions
tug at bed sheets
take shape as
felines and family
dakota people
sleeping
blending their dreams
with mine

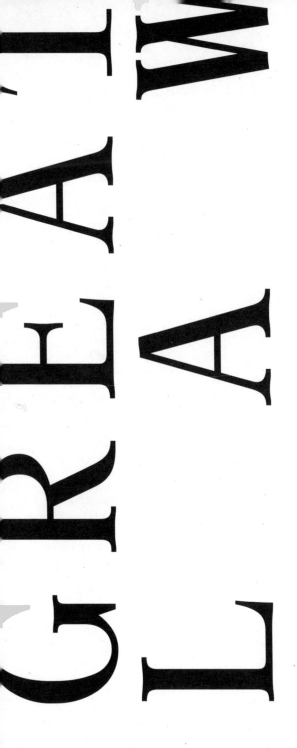

Will you be
my outdoor chief
protect me from negativity
and hold the door for those
intending good

Will you be
my great law story
fight for identity
with great integrity
gift us with
this knowledge
to carry on
and build together
a house of love

Tell me
these territories
are not ours
but belong to
next generations
our purpose is to
leave this earth better
and we remember
we are equipped to keep
it intact

Will you listen
when clan mothers
give the final word
they say
we are done with negotiations
we are taking
our rights and domains
this work we do
with our say so

Will you wait for me
at the bend in the river
where soldiers
are trained in all things
opposite of our existence
I will come to you there
to recover all that is ours
get in the boat

If you look for war
it is war you will find
intelligence and justice supports it
we adopt the message of peace
and protect our people
from those who don't

Will you be
my indoor chief
defend the defenseless
in words and deeds
if you ask the questions
you must be prepared
to sit and listen
long long sessions
for answers to be offered
this is not the Internet

Have you come from
the neutral tribe
are you negotiating
non-compliance
who has brought you here?
and what is your business?

Outside speakers
shorten our language
communication is of utmost
importance
the great law requires
we understand each other
repeat what I say
and keep it correct

Stand on the other
side of the fire
and reflect back
lessons of your own
don't worry about
particularities
all versions
are right
go ahead
add to this truth

Can we reaffirm
this relationship
with patience and persistence
will you be my
walking symbol
of wampum laws
built on peace and clarity

Can you be
my bodyguard
of sorrow remind me
we are family
we are related
together we do powerful
work just look
our crests are not
crowns but emblems
of nature and animals

Can you build
this house with me
and keep room
for expansion
like tree roots
that continue to grow and spread
our minds will follow suit
we know a generous law
evolves with the people
and never loses
its concepts

Will you clear my tears
my throat and ears
the work of recovery
comes with determination
not forced but adopted
into muscles and tendons
with good minds
great minds

This is our law

LAURA SECORD

sacrifice
how I hate the word
no one knows
another's
only motives
be they true to me
or false to you
confidence is inconsequential
to do that which needs doing
remembering
reminding
others too
distinctions between
rights and less than

triumph
is a woman
using the same
tools of oppression
to fowl up the natural
course of destruction
I've eaten my fear
many times over
I've pushed past
exhaustion
and followed
trusted stars
to find my place
where purpose was waiting

wits and guts
cover me like a coat
I walk with choice
in gilded shoes
and carry war's burden
like an orphan between
my breasts
I sleep with grief
of loss and still
live unchallenged
I am holy
as holy as the sun and moon
no petition necessary
for my recognition
if you are standing free
on the riches of your lands
then I can say I have done
something

america
this is how I salute you
my weak once removed name
sits absent from your books
no matter
I write my own
as true confessions
a tyranny survived
I can not deny my destiny
I had no choice
I slayed the enemy in me
and pass a blood stained
sword
to allies on the other side

blessings
there is no sacrifice
but opportunity to
birth a kind of
spontaneous reaction
one of inspiration
for others to follow
do right by natural law
and watch
the most calculated
plans of man
twist into painful
concessions
yes this is of my doing
again and again

tear it down to build it up again
that's money
trickster's gift
transforming into many
what do you do with yours
it's plenty
money
is a joy
and a mutha-fuck'n burden
you gotta have it
can't get through life without it
save money
everyday money
wake up make love to your money
leave this world
leave your money
daddy didn't give me any
left me with riches in skin
deep dark blood lines
who you gonna get with
do they got money
love can't be bought
or be sold to
get what you need to get
do what you need to do
earn it lose it
go choke on it for all I care
low life vibrations
chas'n dollar drama
always on the phone
yell'n curs'n
getting all sweat'n
over simplify'n
paper bags full'a
fast cash
blood money
guilt money
richness is a sickness
crazy lazy vain
blow out your brains
disease distress
fake mistakes
eat it all up
big fat north americans
gorg'n for more
mak'n dollars make sense
like Lillian Allen says:
give a bit to community
but make sure you get yours
manage your numbers
like stock cars coming back round
financial gain
bugs crawling in places you can't scratch
hatching plans to get rich quick
never enough
I want more
poor pour it all over
make it rain out the window

"Hi we are live
in the studio with the one and only Money.
Welcome, tell us a bit about yourself."
"My name is dollar bill.
I come from the land, I come from air
I come from the mind of man."
"Not the heart?"
"No never the heart here
I just want to say today
please stay calm
I will come to you
you don't have to chase me down
I see your dreams, your dreams of winning
I see your dreams, your dreams of living
there is only a fraction I can make happen
a dream a dream double-dog dare to dream
you are the superhero, not me."

HOW DO YOU SAY MONEY

everything on TV is money someth'n
donations in dollars sent to christians
dibbed out to brown ones street ones abandoned
ones
bankrolls buy bedrolls
I love me some US currency
so dirty so worth the exchange
it's not trickery really or sorcery scary
it's greedy greed greedy greed
you know me like no one else money
cabbage, candy, junyah, wistah, *do-re-mi* baby
I see your standards and morals slipping
come and get some
let me fix you up a cuppa
love you and leave you
crave me I'll breed you
sing money songs it changes everything
stand it high on pedestals
pin it on witnesses and send it dancing
round the room
the more you get the more you crave
money makes the man
keeps you coming back
for that smack
that silly dollar bill
paper mâché piñatas
take a wack at it
give it all you get it
fortunes rain
candy scramble
open palms
crawling on all fours
I. Want. More.
   I want it all
   it's all I want
   give me more
   give me all you got
get ambitious get afraid
overstanding the game
trade waits money complicates
nothing at all to do with L O V
everything to do with G R E E
serves us right to fight
when we know
worth is worthless
money-hungry
hungry-money
gold digg'n
try'n steal'n your meal ticket
so innocent these scratchy numbers
come up as hard evidence
true to only you
all the moneys
can't find answers
for cancers
or stop people
fall'n from on high

Black Friday and Apologies
you know the old saying
you can't take it with you
money evaporates when you do
Mu-lala, La-lala, lala, la
a dollar figure appears with every new born
now if that ain't human trafficking...
activity above the radar
government sanctioned bullet-proof investments
fiscal tracking system
a revenue generated GPS
not to be too cliché
but money can't buy you happiness
what it can getcha is a whole lotta sex
poverty is one letter away from poetry
go ahead get naked
put it in a pile and jump in it
smell that money
so you don't forget it
it puts the OW in power
the leash in pleasure
come and get your bread and cheddar
spirit and commerce
collide inside the holy Casino
where magic grandma hands
sweep across machines making connections
praying is one letter away from paying
in faith for answers to come pouring onto
motion-sensitive floors in cha-ching bling boing

Ah-Ho!

we have a **bingo!**

no ancestral line
to stretch for that which
exists eternal
reaching from all
directions defined imagined
and not yet known
simple as empty space
complex as a cluttered world
it is breath
grazed against
tension raising vibrational
something
what!

it isn't love or hate
we find our voice
with it and with it
we hear our sonic selves
living tonal emotional
transformational
constantly fighting against silence
being silenced
expressions from lovely
people planting sounds
joining nature and natural vocables

Breath. Sing. Air. Trill.
Sound. Call. Voice. Yell.
Say. Hear. Receive. Speech.
Speak. Tell. Move. Tune.

signals and psychic taping
alerting frequencies
joining forces and airwaves with others
listening
receiving take heed
revealing
what!
life-forces influencing barometers
why resist audio insistence
melodic deliverances
is this not spirit from whence we came
soul-starved nations
of vapid fast convulsive
impulses
keep up
no slow down
dispossessed voices coming at you
Hello!
yelling at you
Hello!
doesn't anybody even live here anymore

walkie-talkie
hi-fi transmitter
terrestrial messages
flying like stars across the sky
wireless whispers
and answers

all tuned in
to different stations
trying to speak
the same language
grotesquely forcing our frequencies
to collide
announcements and advertisements
invisible and expensive
too harsh for tender thoughts
disruptions of our regularly scheduled
programs to bring you these important
what!

sound validations
like hearing your own
laughter listening to yourself cry
say it in your own voice
its fine
like it lick it
bring it to the table and serve it
say what's been said
in a way it's never been said
the way you heard it
but different

simulcast transmissions crossing
channels and creating static
where voices are invisible and colourful
happiness cannot be lost
inside discomfort of diffusion

THE   SPIRIT

I am radio
I am voice and aural territory
with citizens of sound and song
do not adjust your dial
just raise the wire
internal antennae picks up
russia
what!
earthbound sound clips
digital
what!
blips and bleeps
just listen
tell me what
I am speaking
frightened and erratic responses
to drunk love requests
hearing the slurring
I am flipping
frequencies
searching for clarity
hoping to hear
her voice again

airwaves waiting
staying on course
we conclude another broadcast day
imperfect sound grates
like a torrent of lies
something doesn't feel right
hardened atoms no longer
reproduce inspiration
volumes of dead resonance
corn stalks standing still

we've spilled all our secrets
and there is nothing new
so be silent
let the language come to you
voice and space
wrapping the land like a blanket
testimony to time truth
trauma reverberating up and out
healing and hearing
beneath earth's surface
currents above obvious
being told who we are
listening and questioning
surviving weak signals
riding the dials
parting the particles
making our own waves
with sensory assaults
long distance moon in scorpio
static and tensions
go ahead caller
you're on the air

Double Buffalo Double Buffalo
Flap Shuffle Step
Heel toe Heel
Back Essence
Spank Step (cross behind)
STEP Step, Brush
Swing, CHUG Lift
Swing CHUG Brush
Heel Drop Slide Heel Lift Slide
Step Step Step
Cramp Roll
Step Step Heel Heel Toe
Double Cramp Roll
Stamp
Cramp
Roll Turn
Pull Back Pull Back
Shuffle Shuffle
Double Buffalo
Tatanka
Tatanka
Over The Top
Riff Riffle
Scuff
Scuffle
Shirley Temple
Call Your Mother
Ring Ring
Double Irish
Double Scotch
Broth and Brush
Tap Heel Slide Drop
Tap Heel Slide Drop
Lift Jump Lunge
Lift Jump Lunge
Paradiddle
Step Riff Heel
Beat Riff Walk
Crinkle Nose
Smile
Pull Back Pull Back
Time Step
Goes Like This

Slam
Slap
Slide
Smack
Spank
Stamp
Step
Stomp
Time Stop
Single Traditional
Double Triple
Single Travelling Time Step
Shuffle Step Shuffle Ball Change Ball
Shuffle Step Shuffle Ball Change Ball
Again
Toe Tip Toe Stand
Toe Trench
Touch Touch
Waltz Clog
C'mon Again
Riffle Ripple Slurp
Paradiddle Burp
Step Hop Heel Drop
Riffle Ripple Slurp
Leap Jump Brush Scuffle
Scuffle Scuffle
Syncopation Syncopation
Step Hop
Scuff Brush
Bring It Home
Here We Go
Double Buffalo
Flap Shuffle
Spank Step
Step Step
Cross Behind
Swing Foot Slide
Swing Foot Slide
Stamp Cramp
Roll Turn Roll Turn
Wave Turn
Roll Turn
Wave Turn
Tada!

My mother left this world as I entered.
I was Daddy's princess from the day I was born.
At the end of the 1500s we roamed.
We wore little to distinguish our social standing.
Creator could see who was who was who.
And that was all that mattered.
It was true I changed names
Pocahontas to Rebecca.
A consensual reinvention.
My innocence protected.
But they still came.
I saw my first white man at age eleven.
I remember the day.
My father gifted me animal skin leggings.
My stride was plenty wide heading out to fields
looking for delicious dandelions crunchy sweet clovers
anything to bring back to camp as women did.
I watched the mothers packing babies on their backs.
Young playmates changing from girls to grown women.
I only wanted to stay this age.
I only wanted to play.
Too many chores for grown-ups.
Firewood gathering, house building, food growing, preparing and serving
teaching, childbearing, fire keeping, weaving, washing, pot making
carving, meat processing, lovemaking, hide tanning, harvesting,
water hauling, sewing, child rearing, going to sleep and doing
it all again.
His name was John.
My uncle captured him.
Showed him off like a prize
his captured captain.
Offered him to my father this
blue-eyed British.
Foolish is what they called him.
Famous he and I became.
Together but we were never together
in that way.
He tolerated me that is all.
I teased him but cared not.
My father seeing no need for him
wanted to bash his head in
and asked my permission.
No father let him go.
Are we not to be kind to those
seeking survival as we do?
This man has two legs
two arms like us
let him live.
Let him live among us.

P
O
C
A
H
O
N
T
A
S

We adopted him.
And the stories that came forth hence
were fiction and folly.
Drama and disaster.
I was the great child ambassador
sent to make many trades and
negotiate with his people.
Several times and several times
it was good.
A grand conciliation
of newcomers and the original.
I was the intoxicating elixir to their
common and hostile ways.
Everyone got what they wanted
after the visits I paid.
Then greed a sort of expectation
of provisions came as demands.
It was my father's best thought
to leave them to their fate early on.
We had no need to engage.
They offered nothing to compensate.
Daddy's plan was to retreat into the forest
and ambush them in sleep.
But Mister Smith pulled me aside
and having never told a lie I gave him truth.
He and his then fled from us.
Running quick back to their ships.
I have to admit I was glad to see them
take their leave.
Several years passed before I would see
those men again.
I married a young man my father knew and
approved.
I lost nothing in the union.
My princess crown only grew.
Lived with him but maintained my own council.
Freedom was my constant companion.
It was my nature so naturally I would come and
go
and commune with whom I'd choose.
How was I to conceive of the evil
to befall me.
Taken as hostage upon
A British ship captured for ransom.

The price was guns and the release of their
own men.
Gifted with special status and blessed with
girlish charm I was spared harm and taken
instead
to the land they called mother.
I was presented to their queen.
A woman who shone with stones
of every colour.
She sat with her sadness
upon a golden throne.
Never a true friend did she know.
My compassion turned confusion
watching people living every day
against their own nature.
Did they never know freedom?
My heart was touched
by a widower in mourning.
He taught me his tongue
and brought tobacco to my people after we wed.
A strange ceremony would call me
by another.
I no longer was regarded as princess
or special.
I did this for love?
I would never know my father's love again.
As my mother did I had but one child.
Thomas a son.
He would be the great keeper of peace
between our people.
A grand task for such a little boy.
So Mister Disney, you see in the end
I did marry an Englishman.
Not the one you made millions from.
I died at twenty-one.
For the sequence of events
was as natural as stars taking shape
in the sky.
Disease follows trust mistreated.
My death was wretched
but expected.
Living amongst the others
and trading my honour
for a place amongst them.

ANTECEDENT

he said Turtle
she said Wolf
I think Bear
they don't know
saying our names
and all the names
naming those who came
and made me
in time and space
placing flat hands
in the middle of the back
to gingerly push
reluctant clans to the fore
I am their offering
I am the medicine
they left behind
and they tend
with attention
the fire they started
accept deep
agreements
inside me
walk in this skin
show them I am here
I am sister
to them
they are ancestor
to me
we are breathing
in unison
the same medicine
given
in the beginning

winter sun rises
thirty minutes behind
before the first face appears
woman smiling
not seen in years
answers float above
the crust of untouched
snow-filled fields
it's me again
historical provincial parks
closed no access till spring
keep rolling at a hundred
sitting with hours
road sorrow
and headaches
we really don't need
all these signs
to tell us
how much
farther
or symbols of
empty stretches
forced eyes straight
searching
excruciating
feeling
hopeless
sleep-deprived
they say stay with us
when we wake
there at the end
of another day
close as they can
without breaking
the veil
hold our shoulders
touch our backs
extracted emotions
equal to timber leaving
territories as resources
these are not
romantic trees
with sentiment
running beneath
missing their sister
one hundred thousand
for information
validation and rewards
this landscape is white
in January
this landscape is white
in July

travelling away from
geographical centres
tracing perimeters
where town meets field
she has become
a sticker
that follows the back
of vehicles making circles
I follow my own highway of tears

they have all transformed
to deer
bounding out from
trackless banks
standing smack dab
centre
saying
hello I am here
making brief appearances
for remembrances
before sunset again

blackbird chooses
the highest branches
and what she sees
are visions
refusing to come true
spirit uses
light and truth
to track their way
through unchartered trails
busting myths comes
easy as patience
time as ally
holding out
looking over
frozen lakes
I reflect on lessons
you left me
the way you told me
to find my way
and I did
from where we both
hold space now
no wordy celebration
is necessary
it just is

do you remember summer
a lake home
historic and corrupt
dishonest currents
run and touch
the shores where
you were so proud
to pose
no mistake or misfortune
but condition
a feeding frenzy
a fucking zombie
apocalypse
waterbodies abused
delinquent offspring
of Great Lake relations
churning innocence
to the bottom
her story
turned to a tortuous
legacy for a mother
our relations with
those regions changed
now and forever more
I'll visit again
another lifetime perhaps
and wonder what discomfort
is found here
seemingly no reason
this injustice rains
upon us constant

celebrating endings as beginnings
holding our breath
we never breathe
out
memory exists
in the respiratory
a heavy heaving
healing
catching our breath
next time it happens
never letting go
go

listening
is ritual
hearing the ominous
flutter of feathers
passing in opposite
directions
makes us wonder
who is next
point to the part
on your body
that is
home
how
does it feel

a sickness un-arrested
trashmen
looking for new
places to dump
the bodies
don't worry
the lives of those
they've chosen
more than make up
for soul-depletion
they keep going
this is privilege
gone insane

no jackrabbits
in the snow
only tracks
no more birthdays
only anniversaries
no more memorial markers
along highways
they wait
for us
to let them in
the windows of light
so brief
they pass
we move back
under overcast
constant and conscious
I resist
speeding
I must see this
slow down
and feel this
the road has a story
and it is telling us
to witness
fence posts
can't hold
anything
we have adopted
each other
and adapted
to living
like this

BEARS
REPEATING

R E C
L E S

reckless   ness
exists
in creation
random
and
spiritual   esque

uprooted
wanderers
wondering
why

earth's   purpose
                           can take lifetimes
scanning
for answers
to understand

consider   advancements
in reality
and   embrace
embarrassments

found   there
this is as far
as we've come

in dis   owning
cultural ego
we   see
what
it can be

unattended   traditions
lead   to
DE generational
erosion
posing   posturing   sculpted

counter   advancements
identities
still struggling

definitions   articulations
hollywood
moccasins

ruins of their people
was all they saw
the resilience of the natural world
we could not ignore
a territory defined
by hours on foot
we name place in language
and regional reference
a history here in years
counted on two hands
those who dreamed this into being
require guides to find the end
taking river clay to build
power places important to
sophisticated societies
with churches universities
and parliaments
banks built from banks
we all end up in museums
eventually

nothing is considered
without the ability
to see themselves within it
we are non-demanding
but commanding a presence
not controlling but
constantly managing place
the river is straightened
the female source forced to do as she's told
we feel the cessation of natural flow
and witness interference and wonder
the expressway named after the water
the water named after the man
who no one remembers
we doubt authenticity
like too many cosmetic surgeries
nipped and tucked into another
creature entirely

they say no one owns it
they are exposing themselves
through common experience
we remain silent
they are struggling
with articulation
not crossing bridges
obeying signage
we see future activity
believing artist concepts
and planting the visions
with him
they can't stop talking
in sacred spaces
calling it connecting
researching everything
we are putting sumac
in our mouths and tasting
bitter citrus not feeling
a need to compare it to anything

abandoned boot
a hat a blanket
nests and hives
beaver dams in the making
ignoring archived information
comments on brown/grey conditions
we wander onto mud flats
and leave offerings for the honour

one hour
gets you three miles
five kilometers
saved from development/decay
nature and place
place and time
and us and they

416

warm light
white marble
seven o'clock kitchen counter
satisfying time
visiting with guides
in wordless
conversations
they watch
without questions
standing at the window
looking north
observing
absent of judgment
business and education
graduates and planners
returning bringing
western gifts
there is another place
and time remembering
omitting specifics
keeping the heart calm
emotional memory
confrontations around every corner
the feelings stay nameless
not nostalgic
but numb
for the many times
escaping death
when death should have
by rights won
I have come
humble to give thanks
offer a hero's hello
seeing old scenes
played again by others
finding no need
to stay longer

YONGE

I am listening
to an angry man
on the corner
shouting
    "Go to hell to hell with them all."
no way to ignore him
sense eludes him
sometimes sound bites
follow me
I consider them
until the wind lifts them
and music returns
as urban groans
and city squeals
this struggle is real
we are the angry man
screaming on street corners
attempts to be heard
take up all our time

by looking
we are speaking
while passing
counting our paces
joining the masses
saying something
in motion
this is not connecting
but acceptable
communication
it is ancient
it is the foundation
of freedom
freedom to say Yes
freedom to be silent
remain self-reliant
and design individual
futures born from
telepathic transmissions
this is not failure

there is an angry man
on the other line
refusing further calls
he prefers long distance
crucifixions
doesn't speak but
abuses words using all capitals
deletes their meaning
when confronted in person
this man is perfect for the job
slinging insults and accusations
just shy of aggression
colouring within the lines
of professionalism

the quietest spot in the city
is on top of the tallest building
a vantage point of choice
the train will slow
as it passes
so if you want to get on it
you have to jump
one man's passive
is another man's active
respect can be measured
by how long they make
you wait
turning 30 is a choice
if you get there
you'll know it

AND

stay humble
and ask for advice
when entering troubled waters
make sure to wear turquoise
there is a time to sing
and a time to receive
there is a time to learn
and a time to teach
sometimes we fall
so we can hear
the earth better
just remember
stay human

COLLEGE

THIS
IS A
POEM
FOR
NINA
SIMONE

gifted Queen
we've seen
your divine
complexity
your journey
our journey
a woman craving
freedom at all cost
she had to be
what she be
quality
musical magic
emitting from
strong black fingers
a force set on course
mysterious source
born into broad nose
and thick lips
proclaiming her beauty
despite the civil sixties
Miss America North Carolina
didn't see you coming
didn't want you
to leave
all the classical notes
toted and trotted off
making a new place
landing strips for relationships
prospecting constantly negotiating
her talent would not
be denied
fallen from the sky
and play
was all she wanted to do

Eunice now Nina
meaning little one
little nothing
none of what she done
could possibly be ignored
all the pedestals are yours
the house – yours
the floor – yours
behind doors
unnatural acts
the Queen is beaten
bloody bleeding
from the face
her man perpetrating
the unforgiveable
THIS
is the shift
the minor's rock hammer
chipping away
a woman's dignity

until it flips
and leaves for good
right and wrong
no longer hold hands
a strange reality moves in
sanity moves on
her songs become
empty urns
soulless offerings
demons are listening
lifting lightening
from the mouth
striking and dissolving
soft places of solace
a daughter
inheriting hardness

"Don't cry."
"I won't cry."

lessons learned
from the back of the hand
love what is it?
if not pain
confusion and control
no, Miss Simone
you forgot about freedom
like a balloon slipped from your grip
your songs are desperate
keeping you separate
forgetting what you said

"I am black
and I am
beautiful."

FINAL

answers are coming
clear like confessions
for years reasons
why equations
continue to confuse
from indigenous POV
using all the laws
brought here and agreed upon
for what is just and fair
to feel good about ourselves
regain our right to identity
at least request respectful relations
reconciliation means respecting
individual healing
no more mind raping
and discriminating
holding report cards
turning the keys together
reconnecting to our lands

REPORT

trust
what is that?
partnerships
who do you mean?
advocates and champions of change
gotta lotta work to do
seven flames moving circular
representing sacred teachings
Truth
Humility
Honesty
Wisdom
Respect
Courage
and
Love
what is that?
we have all been touched
more so by some
coming to conclusions a survivor's blood
is in you
we hold the true virtues
unlike those we've learned
this truth looks like booze-soaked
gags silencing languages
it takes whole villages
to lift us and reveal
intentional forced christian indoctrinations
cruel abusive education
teaching nothing

and those who died were buried
victim sickness cycling through
absorbing the enormity
through unsuspecting generations
make your promise sacred
never rejected but action plans
to follow
the money was wonderful
but was it really?
speaking from experience
these legacies
put in place as proof of strength
tired of exercising resilience
we are the riches of this nation
and we want ours
how many 94 recommendations
completed and how seriously
will it be taken?
the tears of a prime minister
won't wipe away racism
there is still plenty of road
to travel before overarching
understanding and embracing
collective histories
what appears to be
the end is only the beginning
bringing clarity validation
unearthed stories till everyone
feels the trauma

our resistance
resisted
word-laws
unfamiliar and evil
why we kept asking
seemed no reason
cruel conclusions
our hearts together feeling
collective confusion
stopping blood pumping
clotting the flow
transplanting answers
with negligence
uncertain future
knowing knowledge
is power
the taking of
effecting me
and everyone after
with this affliction

M
H

little more to say
we silently remember
looking for dignity
not appearing in
who we are now
disappointments reverberate
our namesakes
play with disobedience
gut-knowing goes ignored
never again
we know better
than to abandon
we are reclaiming minds
and reteaching
not only ours
but everyone

S

H

E

L

were there only us
we'd drown in the illusion
of our own importance
spill blood over the ridiculous
and pray to vaporous sources
paying in faith with little return
we are saved by sources
beyond ourselves
strange yet real
rejecting simple notions
animal/mammal-like man
forest beings exacting
necessary survival practices
our reflection relations
maybe once and twice
removed

stealing away
to dense dark dens
set high on hills
foot traffic limited
impossible mortal accessible
important territory
untouched
unaffected by frost fog
gorging on seasons
of buffet changes
they answer
only to each other
in violent clashes
log messages and innate languages
only spoken only when
necessary

no waste
it is how they get away
no trace
but the silent DNA
askew to human
what are they what is it
how do they exist
and yet not
make us believe
in a presence
with more questions
than evidence

dampened answers
pass under microscopes
we have fallen in love
with mysterious
the illusive promise of other
cease to chase but place
invitational objects
stacked along thick
bush paths
rope
perfectly shaped stones
long solid branches
and something
we don't know
what

free
of us
only curiosity
and perceived protocols
provide hope
we want to be first
first look
first to peel
back all doubt
hold evidence and proclaim
there is something
bigger
than any question
stranger
than any truth
more magnificent
than fiction

this thing of rich stories
retold and compared
from safe places
off road over tea
remembrances evoking
guttural swelling sounds
backgrounds and theatre
of the mind
sonic thrill rides

' TO : WANE

THE BIG
FOOTED ONE

"I was driving home.
It was a cold October night.
My wife by my side
dosing and waking.
Roads slick and empty.
Large black creature passing.
Bolting us to attention.
Images seared into memory
from oddity and fear."

'Hey dead, did you see, that?'
She said 'Ya.'
We ceased to speak
more of it."

what do we call it?
how to communicate with it?
these living petroglyphs
keeping all their secrets
leaving us to project
our values
and evidence-less speculations

so many names
Sasquatch
Bigfoot
B'gwas
Chuchuna
Devil Monkey
King Kong
on and on
from A to Z
in every country
for something beyond

three days of listening
three days of writing
imagining what's inside
Sasquatch pouch
big foot purse
not bus tickets
not bubblegum
not paper clips or hairpin
rather fish skins
braided grasses
ointments and oils
pebbles with symbols
weeds and flowers
all the tiny flesh inheritances
of their beloveds
not unlike us
keepers of things

living in legends
breathing in time-traditions
we produce them
from air so thin
to where they disappear
mountain-cousins
rivers and cliffs
exist with freedom
so envious

BE
AR
LO
VE

my medicine
is love
buried
my buried
love
loves to be
buried
safely sitting
unemotional
controlled
escaping
through eyes
where it climbs
to find
light
and like
the sun
the stars
and all
celestial movements
it shines
from inside
unspoken
yet expressed
my medicine
is love
and looks like
respect
when we come
together
it's proper
to keep
distance
and with
authentic
connections
the bear inside me
stands facing you
extending my heart
my medicine
is a bear
coming out
of hibernation
into new seasons
of equinox celebrations
bonfires and firecrackers
sparklers and lanterns
birthday cakes
with a hundred
candles burning
my medicine

ROOOOOOOAAAAARs

good morning
it listens
when birds begin to sing
they tell us
let it out

     let it out

        let it out

           ## let go

Janet Rogers is a Mohawk/Tuscarora writer from the Six Nations territory, living as a guest on Coast Salish territory since 1994. She is a recording artist, former Poet Laureate of Victoria, the University of Northern British Columbia Writer-in-Residence for 2015 and the Ontario College of Art and Design NIGIG Visual Culture Visiting Artist in 2016.